Investigating Science with Coins

by Laurence B. White, Jr.

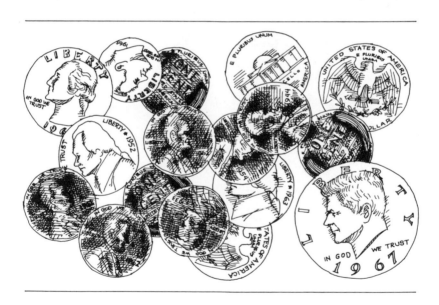

 Addison-Wesley Publishing Company

Reading, Massachusetts

To my wife Doris
and my sons Bill and Dave

Books by Laurence B. White, Jr.

Investigating Science with Coins
Investigating Science with Rubber Bands
Investigating Science with Paper
Investigating Science with Nails
So You Want to be a Magician?

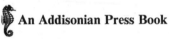 **An Addisonian Press Book**

Illustrations by Will Winslow

Text copyright © 1969 by Laurence B. White, Jr.
Illustrations copyright © 1969 by Addison-Wesley Publishing Company, Inc.
All rights reserved
Addison-Wesley Publishing Company, Inc.
Reading, Massachusetts 01867
Library of Congress catalog card number 69-15796
ISBN: 0–201–08654–9
Printed in the United States of America
Second Printing

HA/HA   8/73   08654

Table of Contents

1	Start with This One	5
2	Coins in Your Eye	8
3	Money Metals	29
4	Coins in Motion	43
5	Math Magic with Money	60
6	Final Fun-damentals	80
	Index	93

1

Start with This One

It's surprising how much you can learn just by having fun ... and how much fun you can have with just a little learning. For instance, can you tell when a glass is full of water? If you think that's a silly question, the results of this investigation will surprise you!

Fit Ten Pennies in a Glass Filled with Water

Things Needed:
Ten (or more) pennies
A glass full of water

Be sure that the glass is completely filled. It should be so full of water that one more drop would cause it to spill over.

Hold a penny edgewise and lower it slowly into the water. Let it fall to the bottom. If you are careful, the water will not spill out. Keep dropping pennies. You will discover that there is room for at least ten pennies in that full glass.

Both water and pennies take up space. If you drop a penny into a glass of water, the level must go up, because two things can't be in the same place at the same time. So if the glass is already full of water, why doesn't it spill when you try to add something else?

The answer is *surface tension*. Water is covered with an invisible skin. Water is made of tiny particles called molecules. Each molecule attracts every other one like a magnet. In the center of a glass of water, every molecule must attract the others which are all around it. But at the surface there are no water molecules above to attract, so the surface molecules attract those that are below and beside them much more strongly. The surface molecules attract each other so strongly that they seem to form a rubber-like sheet.

As you drop pennies in, the water level does rise. But the water does not spill. It bulges upward, much like a balloon bulges when air is put into it. If you look carefully at the water surface from the side, you will be able to see the water bulging higher each time you add a penny. The molecules on the surface continue to attract each other, but finally the bulge becomes too big . . . the strain becomes too much . . . their attraction is too weak . . . and the skin breaks!

Now how would you like to trick a friend? Give him ten pennies and a glass full of water, and you take the same. Show him how to put the pennies in the glass, then challenge him to fit more pennies into his glass than you did.

To be certain of winning, all you need is a tiny bit of dishwashing detergent soap. Before your friend arrives, rub a *tiny* bit of the detergent on two or three of his pennies.

Why will this assure your winning? Detergent soaps contain an ingredient called a wetting agent. This chemical lessens the surface tension on water. It lowers the attraction of the surface molecules, so there will be no skin to hold the water together. It makes "wetter water" which gets easily into tiny cracks and spreads evenly over the surface of a dish. For washing dishes, the wetting agent is certainly a help . . . but for filling a glass of water with pennies it is just the opposite. Most of your friend's pennies will not have detergent on them, so he will probably get several into the glass. However, as soon as he drops in a "soapy" one, the wetting agent will break the surface tension and the water will tumble down.

Naturally, if he is a real friend, you will tell him how you did it and give him a chance to beat you with clean pennies. The very best part of a science magic trick is sharing the secret. Who knows, your friend may know a trick of his own, and you'll certainly want to know how he does it.

2

Coins in Your Eye

Have you ever heard that "a picture is worth a thousand words," or that "seeing is believing"? Do you really trust pictures? Can you really trust your eyes?

You have probably seen at least one picture of a tall building, taken from near the bottom of the building. The bottom looks very wide, and the top very narrow. Are buildings really shaped like that? How about a photograph of a person standing in front of a tree? He might look as though he had branches growing out of his head. You know that's impossible! What about a picture taken with the camera out of focus? Was the camera at fault, or was your friend really fuzzy all over?

Your eye can be compared to a camera. It has a lens, and a light-sensitive layer called the *retina*. Your iris, like a camera diaphragm, controls the amount of light that enters, and your eyelid could be called the shutter. Together, they form a photograph that your brain can see. Because your eye works like a camera, it can also give you a faulty picture.

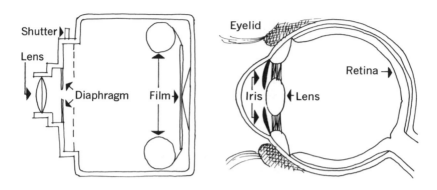

Your eye is much like a camera.

If you set out with your camera, you could deliberately find a dozen different ways to take pictures that would show things completely wrong. Of course, you would have to know something about photography and how a camera operates to do it.

Instead, let's use your eyes as cameras. Your eyes, and a few coins to look at, will convince you that seeing is often deceiving.

IS YOUR BRAIN IN THE WAY?

Your eye is not the only thing you need for sight. It is one of three important links in your seeing chain. Without *light*, you could not see. The first requirement for seeing is that light reflects off the object. The *eye* can then form an image using this light. Lastly, you must use a *brain* to interpret what the image means. If any one of the links is missing, you cannot see. If any one is confused, you cannot believe what you are seeing.

If you looked at a bright red apple in a room with only green lights, the apple would look green. The light would not be reflecting a true image.

When a photographer takes a flash picture of you, you see the flash long after the bulb goes off. Your eye is making a mistake, seeing something that is no longer there.

Your brain is the most deceptive. It can only decide what you see from the information you have given it. Each time you hear, smell, taste, touch, or see, you are providing your brain with facts about your world. If you make mistakes, have not been careful enough, or have not learned enough, your brain may mislead you or even provide you with information that is not true.

Here Are Three Circles

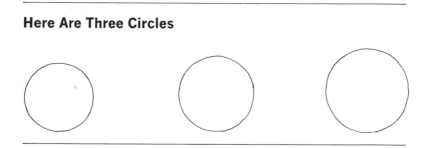

Can you tell which circle is exactly the same size as a penny?

There are two ways to find out whether your choice is right or wrong. The easier way is to take a penny and try to fit it into each of the circles. Your eye can then decide for you. The other way is to let your brain correct itself. At the moment, the only information you have is the picture of the circles and the pennies you have seen. This is information you have given your brain and, with it, your brain is trying to give you the answer. But this is not really enough information for you to be sure of your decision.

With a bit more information, you will be able to decide with confidence which circle is penny-sized. The three circles were made by drawing around three different coins: a dime, a penny, and a nickel. Now you know which one represents the penny! If you guessed right, or even if you didn't, you might want to make up a few cards with these circles on them and give your friends the test. You will discover that many of them will make a mistake.

Have you learned that you should not always trust your brain to recognize what your eyes see? In this investigation, your eyes did not mislead you. A penny would make the same size spot in your eyes as one of the circles, but your brain probably recognizes a penny more easily by color, or by the printing on it, than by size. In this case your brain easily gets in the way of your eye and chooses the circle it thinks is proper, ignoring the spot your eye knows is right.

Scientists have tried tests like this with many people. They have found that poor children will often choose a larger circle to represent a penny than children who always have a pocket full of change. If having a coin were a real treat for you, your brain might easily see coins bigger than they really are.

Your brain will always try to give you an answer. If the information you have is not enough, we call the answer a guess. Whenever we try to decide how big, or long, or far away something is, we are guessing.

To prevent his brain from getting in the way, a scientist does not trust his guesses. He uses rulers, scales, and all sorts of measuring instruments to prove what he is seeing. Often he may be puzzled because his brain and his ruler will not agree, but he will always trust the ruler over his eyes.

Measure with Your Eyes

Things Needed:
Ten pennies
A ruler

Arrange ten pennies in a line on a table so that each one touches the next. Take the eight pennies away from the middle, leaving only the ones at each end. Be sure not to move the end pennies while removing the ones in the middle. Now try to guess the distance between the two remaining pennies. The space is exactly 6, $6\frac{1}{2}$, 7, or $7\frac{1}{2}$ inches. Is this enough information to give you the right answer?

Do you need a ruler to be certain of your answer? With the information you have, the answer is "yes." With a little more information, you could be certain without a ruler.

Look at one of the pennies. How wide is it? Watch out now, you are going to have to guess again, and you will have the same old trouble with your brain getting in the way. If you used a ruler, you would find that a penny is $\frac{3}{4}$ of an inch wide. You know how many pennies you removed from the line, and with this new fact you can readily determine the distance between the pennies without guessing.

You cannot always believe what you see. Size and distance are very difficult to guess accurately. Your brain usually gets in the way and tries to serve you when it should not be trusted. You must always be certain to have all the facts before trying to solve any problem. If the facts are lacking, use a book, a ruler, or any means you can to check your brain before you believe it.

FOOLED BY YOUR FOVEA

What is a fovea? It is a spot on the back of your eye that allows you to see sharply. If you did not have a fovea, everything you see would be blurry and fuzzy. To see clearly, you line up whatever you are looking at so that its image falls right on your fovea. As you read this book, every word must pass right across your fovea. And your fovea is just about the size of the period at the end of this sentence.

It is hard to believe that everything you see clearly must pass across such a tiny spot in your eye. If you

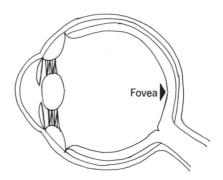

The fovea appears as a tiny dent on the back of your eye.

look around the room right now, you will be sure that everything you see is in sharp focus, but it isn't!

Place two pennies about five inches apart on a table. Concentrate on either one of them. You must really stare at the one you select, and try hard not to move your eyes from it. While you are staring at one, can you read the date on the other one?

You will not only be unable to read the date, but the other coin will be so blurry you will probably not even be able to tell that it is a penny.

Keep staring at the coin you selected. Now reach down and push the blurry one towards it. How close

---

Hocus Focus

Things Needed:
Two pennies

do you have to move it before you can see the dates on
both coins clearly? Does this convince you that your
fovea is indeed very small? It is so small that you
cannot fit the images of two side-by-side coins on it at
the same time.

When you look around, most of the room is really
quite blurry. If you hold your eyes still on one object,
and think about what your fovea does, you will agree
that the only thing in the room that is not blurry is that
one thing you are staring at.

If you look at one object, you are usually so interested
in it that you don't realize, or really care, that nothing
else is clear. In fact, this helps you to concentrate on
what you wish to study. When you look about, your
eyes dart to and fro. Your brain will register a small
clear picture from each of these darting glances, and
from all the pictures it will form a very good mental
image of the room, in great detail. Your fovea works so
well, and so quickly, that you rarely notice how little
you really see clearly.

Because your fovea is essential to clear vision, you
should avoid any possibility of injuring it. Have you
ever tried to burn a piece of paper by concentrating the
heat energy of the sun through a magnifying glass? The
results are a dramatic demonstration of the reason for a
basic safety rule: never look at the sun through a telescope. If you tried to observe the sun with a telescope,
you would have to line the sun up on your fovea. The
heat, concentrated by the telescope lenses, could burn
your fovea and prevent you from ever seeing sharply
again. Then you might have to go through the rest of
your life seeing only blurry pictures through that eye.

Too much or too little light is bad for your fovea. For example, when you read a book, every word passes across your fovea. If you read in dim light, the fovea may be unable to form clear pictures. This may result in eyestrain, which could cause watery, tired, or sore eyes, or perhaps even a headache.

DOUBLING THINGS

A good way to double your money is to put it in a savings account at a bank. You will be paid money (interest) for lending it to the bank, and if you leave it all in the bank long enough, you will have twice as much as when you started. If you are in a hurry, however, you can fool your eyes and see twice as much money, simply by seeing double.

If you had only one eye, you could still see things just as clearly as with two. You can prove this by closing one eye and looking around; you probably won't notice any difference at all. But having two eyes does make a difference to the way you see, as you'll "see" if you try this investigation.

Hold a half dollar roughly half an arm's length away from your eyes. Close one eye and look at the coin. Naturally, you will see only the one coin. Now, before opening your other eye, change your focus so that the wall behind the coin is clear and sharp. The coin, and your fingers, will become blurry, but you will be able to make out the form of the coin. Now return your focus to the coin so that it is again clear.

Open your other eye. You will notice that you cannot really see the coin any better than you could with

Double Your Money

Things Needed:
Half dollar

one eye. Again, change your focus to the wall, this time with both eyes. What do you see now? Have you succeeded in doubling your money?

Each of your eyes makes a separate picture of anything you look at. Both of these pictures are sent to your brain. Your brain blends these two pictures into one, and this is the picture you have of the world. But this still doesn't explain the value of having two eyes.

Your eyes are spaced about two or three inches apart on your face. Therefore, each eye will see a slightly different picture. If an object is in front of your nose, your right eye will see slightly to the right of it, and your left eye slightly to its left. When these two different views reach your brain, you are able to blend the two scenes together and form a single picture in *three dimensions.* Now, everything you look at will have the dimension of width, height, and, thanks to the two pictures, a dimension of depth.

With two different views, you are able to generally decide how big around an object is, what shape it has, and whether it is near to or far from you. You know if a speeding automobile is far enough away for you to safely cross the street, just where your pencil is when you reach for it, and that elephants are sort of round. What kinds of problems might you have if you couldn't see depth?

Reach out and . . .

Things Needed:
A dozen coins

Scatter the coins on a table and step back about an arm's length from them. Bend down so that you are looking at the coins from an angle and some of the coins are farther away than others. Close one of your eyes and keep it closed, and then quickly reach forward and tap each of the coins with your finger. Do this as fast as you can. How many did you miss? How many were not quite where you thought they should have been? Now you can appreciate the advantage of having two eyes; if you had been using both of your eyes you probably would not have missed once.

Of course, two eyes can sometimes be fooled. It was because of using two eyes that you doubled your money. As long as your eyes focus on one object, your brain will blend the two pictures into one. The two pictures cannot be too different, however. When you focused on the wall, the two pictures of the wall blended together perfectly, but the coin appeared in quite a different place against the wall in each eye. Because your brain was blending the far away wall, it could not blend the nearer object, the coin, at the same time. So you were able to see two coins.

Here is one last "double" investigation. When you had both eyes focused on the coin, you noticed that you had a picture of one coin—but did you notice that you also had two pictures of the wall? You will probably need something like a picture hanging on the wall to notice this. Try it again and this time, double the wall!

HALVING YOUR MONEY

Having found a way to make two coins from one, perhaps it is only fair to find a way to see one coin where there are two. Let's look inside your eyes to find out how.

The retina contains tiny light-sensitive cells. You have about 107 million of them in each of your eyes. Chemical changes in these cells are sent as messages to your brain by way of your nerves. Your nerves act like telephone wires, carrying these messages of what your eye sees to your brain.

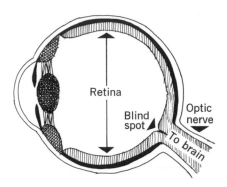

The place in the retina not sensitive to light where the optic nerve leaves the eye is called the blind spot.

All the nerves from these cells leave your eye at one place. This place is toward the back of your eye. Here the nerves gather together and form a large cable, called the *optic nerve*. Not every cell has a fiber in the optic nerve. Some of the cells work together and share one of the nerves. Still, the optic nerve is made of many thousands of nerve fibers, and the place where they leave your eye is very crowded with them. In fact, it is so crowded with nerves that there is no room for any of the light-sensitive cells. Because of this, the place is called your *blind spot*.

Your blind spot is just that—a spot in your eye that cannot receive a picture. Think about this and you may not believe it. Somewhere on this page there are some words you cannot see right now. So the page is somewhat like a photograph with a hole cut in it. The hole is that part of the page which is over your blind spot. You may not believe it because your eyes work in a special way and you do not notice it. If you could see it easily, you certainly would think there was something wrong with your eyes or the book. How can you find your blind spot?

Suppose there was a coin on the table and, as you looked at the table, the image of the coin fell on your blind spot. With no cells there to receive its picture, you wouldn't see the coin. This will be the goal of our investigation.

Before beginning, you must know three things that are important for success. You must use only one eye to keep the image of the coin on your blind spot, you cannot move your eye, and the image of the coin must be small enough to fit on your blind spot.

Place two small coins on a table so they are about three inches apart. Bend over the table so that you are looking down on the coins. Position your head so that it is about six inches directly above the coins. Close your right eye and keep it closed. Now, with your left

---

Find Your Blind Spot

Things Needed:
Two small coins

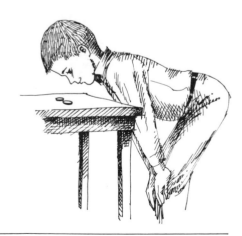

eye open, look at the coin on your right. If you are doing it properly, you will be looking over your nose.

Without moving your eye, slowly raise your head. If you focus sharply on the right-hand coin, the coin to the left should vanish when your head is about a foot away from it. Unless you shift your eye, the coin will be completely invisible. If you do not succeed at first, try it again. The most common mistake is to shift your view away from the right coin. You cannot look toward the left one; you must simply notice that it is gone from the corner of your eye.

Once it does go, you can easily prove that it is still there. Just open your right eye. Your right eye will see a slightly different view. The coin will not be on the blind spot in the right eye, so it will suddenly reappear. Does this explain why you usually see an entire scene without any missing pieces? What one eye misses, the other eye sees. If you really want to see a hole in this page, you must look with one eye closed. Chances are you still won't notice the part that is gone because your eye normally moves back and forth.

How large is your blind spot? It is about as big around as the head of a straight pin. But how much can you fit into it? That's not really a trick question. The further away an object is, the smaller it appears and the less space it will take in a picture. You can easily make an elephant vanish if he is far enough away, using this same trick. If you practice holding one eye still and focused on an object, you will be surprised at what you can make disappear whenever you like.

Try this same investigation with half dollars. Can you make one of these big coins vanish as easily as a smaller one? Do you have to move your eyes further away? Once you have made a coin vanish, hold your eye very still and reach down and touch the missing coin with your finger. Of course, because it is still really there, you can do this easily. But does the end of your finger also disappear? By holding two of your fingers in a V, can you stare at one and make the other one vanish?

PERSISTENCE OF VISION

Your eye works like a motion picture. You know that movies don't really move. They are made of thousands of separate pictures, each just a little different from the previous one. When they are flashed before your eyes, one picture always stays until the next appears. The images of the two pictures then blend together and our brains see this as motion.

Your eyes make separate pictures, too! While your eyes are open, chemicals in the light-sensitive cells undergo rapid change. When they see light, they change, and then they change back as they were. If the light is still present, they will change again. These rapid changes allow us to look at something different or to know if something moves in the scene we are observing.

It takes about $\frac{1}{20}$ of a second for the chemicals to make one complete change. Therefore, just like a motion picture, your eye sees about 20 pictures every second. Naturally it would be quite annoying if you were aware of these changing pictures. Your world would look like a flickering motion picture being shown at too slow a speed. Instead, your eye and your brain will hold one picture until the chemicals complete their change and provide you with the new one.

The scientist calls this "persistence of vision." One picture persists, or stays, until a new one replaces it.

Suppose you could see through a coin. You would see both the head and the tail side at the same time, wouldn't you? You can't actually develop X-ray vision, but persistence of vision can trick you into thinking you have.

Spin a half dollar near a table edge. Watch the coin while holding your head at the level of the tabletop. If

---

See through a Coin

Things Needed:
Half dollar
Well-lighted table

---

you spin the coin very fast, it will probably be just a blur at first. But keep watching it. As it slows down you will suddenly be able to see both the head and the tail at the same time. The illusion will last only a few moments. In these moments, the coin will look very transparent and it will seem to be standing still inside a ball.

Perhaps you can explain what you have seen. If your eye forms a new picture every twentieth of a second, all you must do is cause the coin to turn halfway around every twentieth of a second. Your eyes will first see a picture of the head side. This picture will persist while the coin turns. The next picture your eyes receive is of the tail. Actually, your eye will still hold the image of the head side for a moment after the tail appears, and the two pictures will overlap in your eye. Before you adjust to this, the coin has turned again and the effect is repeated. Although you never actually have both sides facing you at the same time, your eyes truly have a picture of both sides at the same moment.

One and One Makes Three

Things Needed:
Two pennies

Now try this. Hold two pennies, stacked together, between your finger and thumb. Slide them quickly back and forth over one another. Keep your eyes on the edges of the coins. You will suddenly see a third coin appear between them.

Where does the third penny come from? Persistence of vision is again deceiving you. When one penny is down, your eye retains its image in this position. When it slides up, you make still another picture of it here.

The same is happening with the other penny. Your eye holds pictures of the coins in both places, and you see three coins which appear to be standing quite still—two up and one down. The images of the two pennies in the down position persisted in your eye and were joined by your brain to make the extra penny.

Here is a puzzle to solve. Try rubbing a penny and a nickel instead of two pennies between your forefinger and thumb. What do you suppose you will see as the extra coin, a penny or a nickel?

DISTANCE DECEPTION

The sun is almost 1,000,000 miles across. It would require about 500 moons placed side by side to stretch across the sun. But when you look at the sun and the moon in the sky, which one looks bigger? Neither: they look about the same size.

How can something as big as the sun look so small, and something as small as the moon look so big? The answer, of course, lies in their distances from earth. An object closer to our eyes looks larger. We know that our eyes are easily fooled by distance. Before guessing at the size of an object, we often have to know how far away it is.

Can you make a dime as big as a half dollar? Hold a dime in one hand and a half dollar in the other. Hold the half dollar at arm's length and the dime about half as far away. Close one of your eyes and look at the coins side by side. Move the dime closer to your eye, then away. Can you find a place where it appears to be the same size as the half dollar?

Half-dollar-size Dime

Things needed:
A dime
A half dollar

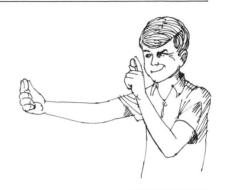

Once you succeed, you can move the dime across in front of the half dollar and easily hide the entire half dollar behind it. In the same way, the moon can hide the sun during an eclipse.

You can fool your friends with distance deception by showing them the most unusual coin collection in the world. The collection is made up of only a dime, a penny, a nickel, and a quarter, and a box. The unusual part is that all the coins seem to be the same size.

The box should be open at the top, to permit you to arrange your collection and to admit light when showing it. Cut a dime-sized peephole in one end of the box. From the other end of the box, make a mark at 7 inches, 10 inches, and $10\frac{1}{2}$ inches on the bottom. Glue a quarter to the end of the box, an inch from the right side. Glue the nickel slightly to the left of the quarter on the 7-inch line; glue it so that it is standing upright on the bottom. Glue the penny to the 10-inch line just to the left of the nickel. Finally, glue the dime to the

World's Strangest Coin Collection

Things Needed:
A dime
A penny
A nickel
A quarter

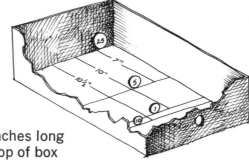

Cardboard box, 15 inches long
Cardboard to cover top of box
Glue

10½-inch line to the left of the penny. If you look in the peephole you should see the four coins, and all will appear to be the same size.

If the coins are not side by side, or if one appears too large or too small, shift positions until they are properly arranged. Then, to prevent your friends from seeing inside until you want them to, place a piece of cardboard over the top of the box.

To show off your collection, ask a friend to look into the peephole, and then uncover the top. Do not let him look down from the top so he can see the arrangement of the coins. Only allow him to use one eye, in just the right place, and then he will become a victim of distance deception.

3

Money Metals

Metal money appeared about 3,000 years ago. At first, unshaped lumps of gold and silver were used. Later, the lumps were fashioned into definite shapes and, still later, they were stamped with designs. Eventually, a flat, round shape with raised designs on both sides became the most common form used for coins.

Gold and silver have always been the most important money metals. Copper, the most common metal found in the United States coins, was first used for coins in ancient Rome over 2,000 years ago. Brass, bronze, and iron have also appeared in coins and, more recently, zinc and nickel.

Surprisingly, the long-time favorite money metal, gold, is no longer used in United States coins. The gold coins that were used by your grandfathers have been replaced by paper bills. However, gold is still the only kind of money used to settle accounts between most nations of the world.

Silver, too, has always been an important ingredient of many coins. A silver coin is not just silver, however.

In its pure form, silver is such a soft metal that you could easily cut a piece with a jacknife. A pure silver coin would wear out in time just from jingling around in your pocket.

All United States coins are made of *alloys*. Alloys are several metals blended together. They are prepared in smelting plants where the different metals can be easily mixed while they are in the molten stage. When the proper amounts of different metals are blended, the resulting alloy will give the best qualities of the separate metals, and will tend to eliminate the less desirable ones. The new metal will be soft enough to stamp with designs, yet hard enough to withstand considerable wear and tear. The coin made from the new metal will make the proper sound when dropped, and it will not rust easily. As you find out about the various alloys that are used in coins, you will readily understand why silver coins are not all silver, a copper penny is not just copper, and a nickel is not just nickel.

A PENNY PARADE

Even the alloys used in the making of coins have undergone many changes, both in the kinds of metals used and in the amounts.

The lowly penny has a remarkable history. To illustrate this, you might enjoy making an interesting collection of pennies. You will have to look carefully through your small change to find them, but a complete collection will consist of *only four pennies*!

What makes each member of this collection odd? Every one of the pennies is a different metal alloy!

Make a Scientific Penny Collection

Things Needed:
A penny dated from 1909 through 1942 or 1946–1961
  (Number 1)
A penny dated 1962 or later (Number 2)
A penny dated 1943 (Number 3)
A penny dated 1944 or 1945 (Number 4)

(Those pennies which you may find hard to obtain can be located in hobby shops which sell coins.)

The first penny (Number 1) on the list is an easy one to obtain because it was the most common kind of penny for about fifty years. It consists of an alloy of 95% copper and 5% zinc and tin. It is the only member of the collection which contains any tin.

Tin is a bright, shiny metal. It is quite soft, easy to roll in thin sheets, and melts at quite low temperatures. It is very durable and is not easily attacked by corrosive chemicals. Resistance to rust and corrosion makes tin a good money metal.

Unfortunately, tin is a very expensive metal. Most tin comes from South America, not the United States. Because it is more valuable for other purposes, and is in short supply, tin was completely eliminated from pennies in 1962.

The second penny (Number 2) first appeared in 1962. It contains the same metals as Number 1, minus the tin. Its composition is 95% copper, 5% zinc.

Zinc is a very old metal. Man has used it for over 2,500 years. Zinc is not a pretty metal, because the bright lustre of a newly polished piece quickly becomes covered with an ugly gray powder. However, this powder does an important job. It forms a "skin" which prevents any further wasting away of the metal beneath it. For this reason, many steel items are dipped in molten zinc to cover them with a rust-preventing shell. This process is called *galvanizing*, and you will find that it shows up a bit later in your penny collection.

Why choose zinc as a money metal? Zinc has long been used to prepare printing plates for the reproduction of drawings and photographs in books. The fine details of a picture can easily be reproduced in the metal. When zinc is alloyed with copper, the new metal is called brass. Brass combines the fine qualities of both metals. It can reproduce the engraving details of coins and still be hard and durable.

The United States' active involvement in World War II began in Pearl Harbor on December 7, 1941. Many different metals for a variety of special purposes were required in the war. One important war metal was soon in short supply: copper. The copper supply was so low in 1943 that all the copper which had been reserved for the making of pennies was "called to war."

The third penny (Number 3) contains no copper. It is the only United States coin made of steel.

Steel is an alloy of iron. Basically, steel is pure iron with just a tiny bit of carbon mixed in. It is a very hard and important metal, but is a very poor choice for a coin. Like iron, steel rusts easily. If steel coins are left in a damp room, they will soon rust, and eventually become corroded bits of metal, unrecognizable as coins. To prevent rusting, these wartime pennies were galvanized with a thin layer of zinc. Thanks to this layer, you may still discover one of the steel pennies, in fair condition, among your change from the candy store.

Another feature of this member of the four-penny collection is that it is attracted to a magnet. The steel penny holds the unique distinction of being the only magnetic coin ever issued in the United States!

Ask a friend to seal each of the four pennies in a separate envelope, noting one penny is silver-colored. He then hands you the sealed envelopes behind your back. After a moment, you hand him the one that con-

Science Magic with Your Four-penny Collection

Things Needed:
Four-penny collection
Four envelopes
Small magnet

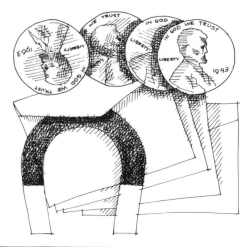

tains the silver-colored penny! How? Hide the magnet in your back pocket. The silver-colored steel penny is the only one it will attract! (Note: Some Canadian nickels contain steel. If you can get one, try your magnet on it.)

Very few metals are attracted to a magnet. Iron and steel are the only metals that are strongly attracted. Nickel is magnetic, but is used in such small amounts in coins that even a "nickel" will not show attraction.

Steel is not a good coin metal. It appeared only as a wartime necessity. The government was anxious to return copper pennies to the people. The last penny in the collection (Number 4) is a halfway penny. It is not a steel penny, nor is it the same copper alloy that had been used before. This penny is a second-hand coin.

Much copper had been used in the manufacture of bullet shells. These shells were brass, which was the needed metal for pennies. Many bullet cases were salvaged and used for making pennies during 1944 and 1945. These pennies are known as "Shell Case Coppers" because of their source.

Do Pennies Come in Different Colors?

Things Needed:
A penny dated 1944 or 1945
A penny made any time
    except 1943–1945
Copper polish
Polishing cloth

Shine the two pennies with copper polish. Is one darker-colored than the other? Which one is shinier? Why? Real brass contains 60–90% copper and 40–10% zinc. The penny usually consists of 95% copper and 5% (or less) zinc. This alloy has a slightly different color and lustre. Penny Number 4 in your science collection will be more like real brass and less like the very special money alloy.

To finish the story, in 1946 the war was over and the penny returned to its copper-zinc-tin composition until 1962, when the tin was eliminated. This returns us to penny Number 2 in the collection and invites us to take another look at the four pennies: fascinating objects for both science and history!

"RUSTY" PENNIES

Many chemicals react with others to form new combinations which are considerably different from either of the original ones. These are called compounds. Water is a good example of a chemical compound. Water is sometimes called H_2O, indicating that it is composed of two parts hydrogen and one part oxygen. Hydrogen is a very light, explosive gas. Oxygen is a gas that is essential for burning. But, joined together as a compound, hydrogen and oxygen form a heavy liquid that puts out fires.

Chances are, if you leave your bicycle outdoors for the summer, you will find it badly rusted in the fall. The metal in your bicycle, when surrounded by moist air, joins with the oxygen in the air and becomes a chemical called iron oxide. The iron oxide appears as a brown scale which flakes off and falls to the ground.

We usually think of iron as the only metal which can rust. Actually, many different metals can combine with other chemicals and waste away. This wasting away is called corrosion.

All the metals in our coins are chosen for their ability to withstand corrosion, among other things, but some of them are better for this purpose than others. Nickel is best and copper is poorest. They are all similar in producing a thin layer of rust on their surfaces which prevents further corrosion.

What does a "rusty" penny look like? Try the following investigation to find out.

Fold a paper towel and push it flat against the bottom of a jar. Pour in enough vinegar to moisten the towel. Place a penny on the towel and screw the cover on the jar. Put the jar aside for about two hours.

You may leave the penny in the jar as long as you wish. The longer you leave it, the more rusty it will

---

Make a Penny Rusty

Things Needed:
A penny
A jar with a cover
Vinegar
Piece of paper towel

become. When you remove the penny, you will find that it is covered with blue-green scale.

Where did this rust come from? Vinegar is a very weak acid called, scientifically, acetic acid. Like all acids, vinegar contains a great deal of hydrogen. The copper in the coin released the hydrogen in the vinegar, which joined with oxygen present in the vinegar to make water. During this chemical reaction the copper also combined with the chemicals in the air in the jar. Sulphur, hydrogen, and oxygen joined the copper to make a bluish chemical called copper sulphate. Chlorine, hydrogen, oxygen, and copper made a greenish chemical called copper chloride. The new chemicals appear quite different from copper, vinegar, and air; yet that is what they are, just combined in a different way. Some of the original copper is now present in these chemicals and, when you clean off your penny, it will have a little less copper. The penny, therefore, has rusted, corroded, or wasted away . . . all words which mean about the same thing.

Clean Your Rusty Penny Like Magic

Things Needed:
Small jar
Rusty penny
Some household ammonia

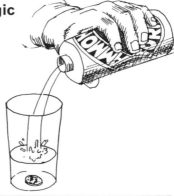

Pour a small amount of ammonia into the jar and drop in your rusty penny. The rust will quickly dissolve and produce a clean penny and a bright blue liquid.

Why does the ammonia clean the penny? Again a chemical reaction is responsible. The copper in the copper sulphate and the copper chloride join with hydrogen and oxygen from the ammonia and produce still another chemical, copper hydroxide.

Repeat the procedure of the rusty penny experiment. No matter whether you use a nickel, dime, quarter, or half dollar, the same kind of rust will be produced. Does this mean that these coins contain copper? Yes. Therefore this experiment can be used as a test for copper. Copper is found in United States coins in the following amounts (percentages vary as alloys were changed):

Nickel, 50% or 75%
Dime and quarter, 10% or 75%
Half dollar, 10% or 60%

Can You Make Other Coins Rusty?

Things Needed:
A coin, or coins, other than a penny
A jar with a cover
Vinegar
Piece of paper towel

IS THERE SILVER IN A "SILVER" COIN?

It is quite unlikely that you will ever find a counterfeit coin. However, if you did, you could be certain that it was not made with silver. You can check your change for possible counterfeit coins and learn a bit of chemistry with this simple test for silver.

Match Test for Silver

Things Needed:
An *old* dime, quarter,
   or half dollar (*before 1965*)
A paper or wooden match
Stainless steel spoon

Place the coin on a table. Light the match and immediately press it against the coin. After the match has burned a moment, remove it, Blow out the match and study the coin. You should see a yellowish spot on the coin. This is sulphur from the match. Leave the coin for a few hours. Does the spot change color and turn black? If so, there is silver present. (Try the same test on a stainless steel spoon to observe the difference.)

Sulphur is used in matches because it burns readily. Ordinarily you cannot see the yellow sulphur because the match heads are dyed different colors.

When sulphur comes close to silver, a new chemical appears. It is called silver sulphide. The silver sulphide appears as a black tarnish on the bright silver.

Much of the silver that is mined is not shiny and bright. You would not even recognize it as silver. It has combined with sulphur from the air and appears dark and dull. Even when polished, silver very quickly tarnishes because particles of sulphur are always present in the air.

Your mother may have a set of silver tableware or a silver coffee serving set. She probably polishes it quite often. When she polishes it, she rubs off a layer of silver sulphide. If you have difficulty in cleaning the silver sulphide off your coin, perhaps you can borrow some of your mother's silver polish.

Mustard Test for Silver

Things Needed:
A nickel, a dime, and a quarter
  dated before 1965
A spoonful of mustard

Smear a bit of mustard on each of the coins. Leave them overnight. When you wash the mustard off, only the coins that contain silver will have black tarnish on them.

This test reminds us that sulphur is a very common chemical in our world. Mustard, like many foods, contains quite a bit of it. If you eat eggs with a silver-plated fork you will find that the fork quickly tarnishes, because eggs contain a lot of sulphur.

We can use sulphur to detect silver; we can also use silver to detect sulphur. Try exposing a silver coin to other things to see if they contain sulphur. To get started, try a rubber band, and then some fruit juice.

Now how would you like to find a nickel that contains silver? Almost all nickels are made of an alloy of copper and nickel. During World War II, however, when nickel was scarce, nickels were made of silver, copper, and manganese. Their dates were 1943, 1944, and 1945 (and some 1942). If you can find one, how can you prove that it contains silver?

If you try any of the above tests for silver with coins dated 1965 or after, you will find that the dimes and quarters do not seem to contain any silver. Do not be alarmed: you have not discovered a counterfeit, because there are some "silver" coins which do not contain any silver at all.

MONEY SANDWICHES

Have you ever seen a "peanut butter quarter"? Chances are, you have spent quite a few of them.

Before 1965 all silver coins contained 90% silver, but several problems developed about that time. The United States just didn't have enough silver to make the required number of dimes, quarters, and half dollars. The size of the coins, and their silver content, had remained the same, but the value of silver had increased. The coins were actually worth more in silver than they were as coins. Something had to be done. A special Coinage Act was passed in 1965 which eliminated silver from dimes and quarters.

A new method was used in the making of these coins. It is called laminating, and the coins are known as clad coins.

Identifying Coins by Touch, Sight, and Sound

Things Needed:
A dime made before 1965
A dime made after 1965

First, compare the two coins with your eyes closed. The coin made after 1965 should feel more slippery than the other and have a somewhat greasy feeling. Study the edges of the coins. Use a magnifying glass, if you have one. Can you find the copper "peanut butter" between the silver-colored outer layers? Drop each coin on the table. Do you notice that each produces a different sound?

The clad dime contains only two different metals, copper and nickel. A thin disk of pure copper makes the central core. Bonded to each side is a special metal alloy made of 25% nickel and 75% copper. The nickel, of course, is responsible for the familiar silver color. The color is about the same, but nickel and copper do not have the same qualities as silver. If you polish both coins in your experiment, you will notice that they have different lustres. Lustre is both the smoothness and the sheen. The clad coin will have a lower lustre due to the high copper content of the alloy.

4

Coins in Motion

Why do things move?
Things move because they are filled with energy.
What is energy?
Energy is the ability to do work.
What is work?
Work is making things move.

Work and motion depend on energy. Energy comes in many different forms. Heat, light, sound, chemical, atomic, electrical, and mechanical energies are the most familiar. All of these can make something move.

Perhaps the most obvious form is mechanical energy. Your mother tells you to "use a little energy" when you are slow to get out of bed in the morning. She is really asking you to show her more mechanical energy. Anything that moves has mechanical energy.

Where does energy come from? How are objects given energy? One easy way is to get it from you.

Lift a coin a few inches off the ground and hold it perfectly still. Does this coin now contain any energy? The answer is yes, even though the coin is not moving.

Energy may be either resting or moving. If energy is moving an object, it is easy to realize that the object "contains energy." Moving energy is called *kinetic energy*.

The coin you are holding, however, has resting energy. The coin doesn't show off the energy at the moment. So we call it *potential energy*. How much potential energy does the coin have? It has enough to move, by falling, all the way back to the ground.

Where did it get enough energy to fall? It got it from you!

You probably ate some food a short time ago. This food grew because of the sun's energy. All animal life depends on plants for food, and plants grow because of the energy they receive from the sun. Heat and light energy from the sun were changed into chemical energy by the plants, and this energy is now contained inside of you. You used some when you lifted the coin. That energy is now in the coin. When you drop the coin, it will be changed into mechanical energy.

The story does not end when the coin drops.

When the coin strikes the ground, mechanical energy changes to two other energy forms, heat and sound.

It is a rather complex story to follow, but it reminds us of two very important rules dealing with energy:

- Energy can be stored by an object, and later show off its presence. We cannot always see whether something contains any energy.

- There are many different kinds of energy. Energy is never lost, but may quickly and easily change from one form to another.

You have watched objects moving all through your life, but you can never really understand how they move until you think about them in terms of energy. Therefore it is reasonable to begin our study of coins in motion, not with a study of motion, but with investigations dealing with energy.

GIVE A LITTLE, TAKE A LITTLE

When you ride your bicycle down the street, you are giving, or transferring, some of your energy to the bicycle. The chemical energy from your food is changed into the useful energy of motion. When you step on the brakes, the brakes get hot. The mechanical energy of the bicycle is changed to heat. It is easy, and necessary, to give and take energy, and to change it to other forms.

In the same way, you can pass the energy along further. If you hit a rock, while riding your bicycle, the rock moves and you stop. The mechanical energy has been transferred from the bicycle to the rock. This, then, is the first rule of energy: it is easy to pass energy from one object to another.

Pass Energy Along

Things Needed:
Ten pennies
Table with a smooth top

Place nine pennies in a row on the table so that each one is touching the next. Place the remaining (tenth) penny about five inches from the row and give it a quick push so that it slides across the table and hits the end of the row. What happens?

You gave the tenth penny a bit of your energy. The harder you pushed the penny, the more energy you gave it. The penny moved. When it struck the first penny in the row it stopped and passed the energy along. The first penny in the row then had the energy. It would move except that there were eight more pennies holding it back, and it did not contain enough energy to move them all. So this penny passed its energy along to the next penny. This one, too, had to pass the energy to the next. Each penny in the row always had other pennies preventing it from moving. Finally the energy reached the last penny. There was no penny to prevent it from moving, so it moved. It contained, and showed off, about the same energy that you gave the original penny.

Move Two Pennies at a Time

Things Needed:
Ten pennies
Table with a smooth top

Set up eight pennies in a row on the table so that each one is touching the next. Place the remaining two pennies about five inches from the row. Making certain that they are touching, give them a quick push so that they slide across the table and hit the end of the row. Do two pennies at the opposite end move, or does just one penny move?

A Quarter Knocker

Things Needed:
Row of ten pennies
A quarter
Table with a smooth top

Place the pennies in a row on the table so that each one touches the next. Place the quarter about five inches from the row, and slide it across the table so that it strikes the end of the row. Will one, or more, pennies be moved?

The heavier an object is, the more energy is required to move it. You would have to work harder to lift an elephant than to lift a dog. The more work you do, the more energy you must use. The more energy you put in, the more energy the object will contain. A quarter is heavier than a penny; more energy is needed to get it moving. Once moving, therefore, the quarter contains more energy and can do more work than a penny.

Now try hitting a row of pennies with a dime. A dime is lighter than a penny or a quarter. What will happen when the dime hits?

THE MORE YOU PUT IN, THE MORE YOU GET OUT

Someone once said that "Life is like a refrigerator . . . you only get out of it what you put in." Energy is very much like that, too. You can only get out of something the energy that you have put in, never more.

The Impossible Penny

Things Needed:
A penny
A piece of string
Sticky tape
Desk with a drawer

Using the tape, fasten a penny on a piece of string and the string to the desk drawer. Using the penny as a pendulum and keeping the string straight, pull it back so that it touches the front of the desk. Let the penny swing free. When it swings back to the desk, does it hit? Can you make it hit the desk if you start it at the desk and do not push it?

A second energy rule, then, is that energy out always equals energy in, never more. If you always start the coin at the desk, it can never go higher. To go higher would require more energy then you gave it.

Does the penny lose its energy? It certainly swings lower on each trip. Energy is never lost, but it may appear to be lost if it changes to another form. *Friction* is a common way by which energy is changed. Friction occurs when two objects rub against one another. What is the coin rubbing against? It is rubbing against the air. Friction with the air is changing the mechanical energy to heat (and sound) energy. The air becomes warmer. Each swing becomes shorter as the mechanical energy becomes less.

If you slide a coin across a table, why does the coin stop sliding?

This is a very serious question. If you give a coin some energy, what happens to it? The energy cannot disappear, so why doesn't the coin continue moving forever? Actually, it would, except it is rubbing against the table. Friction with the tabletop changes the coin's energy to heat (and sound). We can't see heat, but we can see that the moving energy is gone.

When moving energy stops showing itself off, we know it has changed to another form (or forms) of energy.

COINS AT REST

Sir Isaac Newton is best known for his studies of gravity, but the falling apple was only one among many science puzzles he worked out. One of his particular interests was in how objects behave when they move, and when they stand still. He wrote his observations in the form of scientific laws which are known as his *Laws of Motion*. Whether you are studying skyscrapers, automobiles, or coins, Newton's conclusions will apply, because everything on earth follows these same laws of motion.

Newton's First Law of Motion says, in part, that an object at rest will remain at rest, and an object in motion will remain in motion, unless it is acted on by an outside force.   Let's use coins, again, to understand what this means.   There are two rules in this statement. The first states that an object at rest will remain at rest.

Remove the Bottom Penny

Things Needed:
Six pennies
Table with a smooth top

Put five of the pennies in a stack.   Place the sixth penny about five inches from the stack.   To remove the bottom penny in the stack, slide the sixth penny across the table quickly, so that it strikes the bottom of the pile.   It will knock the bottom penny away, but leave the rest of the stack undisturbed.

Why do you think this investigation works?   The stack is the object at rest.   It tends to remain at rest, in one place.   When the sixth penny strikes the stack, it passes its energy on to the lowest coin.   The sliding penny stops.   The bottom penny, now filled with transferred energy, moves away.   The top of the stack, however, stays put.

The word that describes the stack is *inertia*.   Objects stay in place because they have inertia.   Inertia depends a great deal on weight, as you might guess.   It is far easier to get a single penny moving than a whole stack of pennies, just as it is easier to push a roller skate than to push an automobile.

A Weight Problem

Things Needed:
A penny
A dime
A quarter
Table with a smooth top

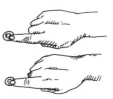

Place the dime and the quarter next to each other on the table. They should not be touching. Place the penny about five inches away. Now slide the penny across the table so that it hits the dime. The dime slides away. Replace the penny in its original position, then try to hit the quarter so that it slides as far as the dime. Does the dime or the quarter have the greater inertia?

More energy is required to move an object which has a great deal of inertia. In the investigation above, you can make the quarter slide as far as the dime, but you have to hit it much harder. You have to move the penny faster, and to do that you use more energy.

Here is another inertia investigation that makes a wonderful science magic trick to surprise your friends.

Snatch the Bill

Things Needed:
A soft-drink (narrow-neck) bottle
A dollar bill (the more worn the better)
A dime

Balance the bill on the mouth of the bottle, and rest the dime on top. How can you remove the bill without spilling or touching the dime?

Hold one end of the bill tightly. With a finger of your other hand, strike the bill downward, sharply, between the bottle and the hand holding the bill. The bill will snap out, and the dime is left sitting on top of the bottle. If you aren't successful with your first try, try again. Remember to hold the bill tightly and to strike downward sharply.

By striking the dollar bill, you are able to remove it before the dime moves. The coin's inertia holds it in place. If you pull the bill slowly, friction will cause the dime to stay with the bill, and it will start to move.

Now try snatching a dollar bill from under a nickel, and then a quarter. Which of the three coins (dime, nickel, or quarter) seems to be the easiest one with which to do this trick? Why?

An Easy Trick That Looks Hard

Things Needed:
A coin

Hold your arm bent at the elbow, with your hand beside your ear. Rest a coin on your elbow. Now swing your arm down quickly and try to catch the coin when it falls off. How does inertia help to make this juggling trick easy to do?

MONEY AND MOMENTUM

Now we come to the second rule in the statement on page 50. Inertia is not only the tendency of an object to stay still. It is actually the tendency of an object to continue doing what it is doing. So, if something is moving along, it will keep moving because of inertia.

Moving things do not seem to keep moving. They slow down and stop. Only in a place where they could not rub against anything, or bump into anything, would they continue moving forever. Outer space is such a place. If you took a rocket into outer space, you would have to use great power to start moving the rocket. But once you were away from the earth's atmosphere, you could shut off the engines and coast on the rocket's inertia.

If you throw a baseball, it will stop when it reaches the ground. Its energy of motion changes to heat (and sound) energy when it hits. The baseball, like any moving object, has a certain amount of energy. The amount of motion is called *momentum*. If the baseball has little momentum, it will make a small dent in the ground when it hits. If it has much momentum, a big dent will result.

Momentum depends on two things. Perhaps you can guess what they are after doing some investigations using coins.

Race against Time

Things Needed:
A penny
A quarter
Watch with a second hand
Table with a smooth top

Before actually trying this experiment, make a guess as to which coin will win. Now, spin a quarter on the tabletop. Count the seconds before it stops. Now spin the penny. Try to give it the same amount of twist you gave the quarter. Time the penny. Which of the coins spun longer? Spin and time each of the coins several times to be more sure of your answer.

The first of the two "magic words" in momentum is *mass*. If two objects are moving together, the more massive one will always have the greater momentum. If a friend threw a table tennis ball at you, as hard as he could, it would be easy for you to catch it; but what if he threw a bowling ball?

Can you see how inertia and momentum go together? A massive object has a greater tendency to remain at rest than a light one does, and therefore a massive object is harder to start moving. It requires a great deal of energy to get going. Once it does start, however, it contains all that extra energy, so it is harder to stop. It has more momentum!

The second "magic word" is easier to guess. Try this investigation.

A Snap, Flick, and Twist Experiment

Things Needed:
A quarter
Table with a smooth top

There are three ways to spin a coin on a table. Hold a quarter flat between your thumb and forefinger and snap them to make the coin spin. You can also rest the coin on edge on the table, holding a finger on top. A quick flick with a finger of your other hand will start the coin spinning. The third way is to hold the coin by the sides and give it a quick twist. Which of these three techniques keeps the coin spinning the longest? Can you explain why one method is better than the others?

If someone were to toss you a bullet, you could catch it easily (though this is *not* a recommended investigation). But if the same bullet were put in a gun and fired, you certainly would not want it pointed toward you. Why not? It is the same bullet, and it weighs the same. But now it is moving at a considerably greater speed.

Velocity, or speed, is important to momentum. To make an object move faster requires more energy. The more energy the object has, the harder it is to stop.

So now we know that the energy of something moving depends on how massive it is, *and how fast it is moving*. Now try to explain, by momentum, why an automobile becomes more and more dangerous the faster it goes.

THE LOW DOWN ON SLOW DOWN

The laws of momentum state that a heavy object will have more inertia than a light one traveling at the same velocity. Occasionally this may not be obvious.

Here is an investigation which might puzzle you because the heavy object, with more momentum, slows down and stops sooner than the lighter one.

Set up two books to form a hill on a floor rug. A rug is important; can you guess why? Lay the quarter flat at the top of the book hill and let it **slide** down. Hold the penny, on edge, then let it **roll** down. The penny will always go further. Why?

The Quarter Loses the Race

Things Needed:
A quarter
A penny
Two books
A floor with a rug

Before you answer this puzzle, perhaps you might try the investigation again. This time, however, **roll** both the quarter and the penny down the incline. You will find that, when they are both rolled, the quarter always beats the penny. With this clue, can you give a reason why the quarter loses when it slides down?

Friction is the bugaboo. Everything is rough when examined under a microscope. The coin is rough, the book cover is rough, and when these rough surfaces rub together, the energy of motion is changed into heat (and sound). When heat is produced, the coin begins to slow down.

A quarter, lying flat, has more surface area in contact with the book than the penny on edge. We can say that more of the quarter rubs against the book than does the penny. Also, a quarter, being heavier, presses down harder, which makes even more friction. It is friction that causes moving objects to slow down and stop. In all experiments with motion, a scientist will keep friction in mind. Frequently, when a moving thing does not behave quite the way we feel it should, friction, even from rubbing against the air, will be the reason. Exact experiments with motion would have to be conducted in a totally empty place, a complete vacuum where there is nothing to bump into and nothing to rub against; outer space is a good example.

Objects can move more freely if friction is lessened. Liquids, such as oil or water, can lessen friction when placed between two surfaces. You could try the sliding race (quarter lying flat, penny on edge) after wetting the quarter with water. The quarter may still lose, but it will probably slide farther than it did the first time.

THE STRAIGHT RULE

Sir Isaac Newton's First Law of Motion includes another rule which we can investigate. Once an object begins moving, it will move in a perfectly straight line, unless something moves it aside.

If you toss a baseball, it should go straight. But it curves downward. This is because gravity moves it aside, out of its straight line path. If you threw the baseball in outer space, it would continue in a straight line and demonstrate the truth of Sir Isaac's rule.

How does an earth satellite travel around the earth? An earth satellite and a baseball behave in much the same way, except that the satellite is traveling faster.

If you could throw a baseball fast enough (about 18,000 miles per hour) it might become an earth satellite. Imagine throwing a ball that fast toward a friend. The ball goes by him and continues in a straight line. Because the earth is curved, the ball would travel away from the earth toward outer space. Naturally, gravity would draw the ball downward. Now it can no longer go straight because gravity is drawing it down . . . but neither can it fall all the way back to earth because it still tends to go in a straight line. The ball must follow a path part way between both forces. The curved path about the earth is called an *orbit*, and in following this path, the satellite is not breaking either the straight rule or the law of gravity.

The next investigation will require some practice. First, make a little tape shelf on the bottom bar of a hanger, right under the hook. Hang the hook on your finger and balance a penny flat on the shelf. Carefully

Why Doesn't the Penny Fall?

Things Needed:
A penny
A metal coat hanger
A piece of tape

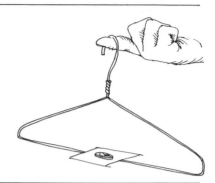

spin the hanger around your finger. With care, you will be able to do this without making the coin fall.

When you spin the hanger, your finger causes it to revolve in a circle. When the motion of the hanger starts the coin moving, the coin tends to fly away from the hanger. The hanger keeps pulling it back into the circle. The coin pushes outward against the hanger.

You might think of the coin as a space satellite, trying to fly straight out into space. The hanger would be gravity, constantly trying to pull it back, moving it from this path. Your finger, of course, is the earth.

The fact that the coin does not fly off the hanger might amaze your friends. A little thought, however, will convince them that all of the objects are following the same science rule that keeps satellites in orbit, the moon circling the earth, and the earth going in a great loop around the sun.

This investigation is a perfect example of common objects following simple rules of energy and motion. It looks mysterious only when we have not taken the time to fully understand the rules.

5

Math Magic with Money

A scientist might make a good magician. Many profes-
sional magicians use tricks which involve science.
Mathematical tricks are especially good, because most
people have difficulty with numbers. It is easy to
confuse, or trick, a friend with ordinary arithmetic and
a little psychology.

Coins make ideal objects to use in math-magic
tricks because they can represent many different
numbers in different ways. Each coin represents a
single unit, or the number one. The values of the coins
are the useful numbers 1, 5, 10, 25, and 50. Each coin
has two sides. The names of coins have different
numbers of letters. Some coins, like the dime, represent
an even number (ten) and others, like the nickel,
represent an odd number (five). Even the dates on
coins can be used as different numbers.

You can use all these numbers to fool your friends.
If you study the principles carefully, you should even
be able to make up a few money-math-magic tricks of
your own.

HOW MUCH CHANGE DOES YOUR FRIEND HAVE?

Would you like to startle your friend by telling him exactly how much money he has in his pocket? Here is a math-magic trick which you can repeat many times without fear of his getting wise.

Your Friend's Change

Things Needed:
A friend with a pocketful of change

Ask a friend to count all his money while you are not looking, and figure out how many cents it is worth. (One dollar and fifty-five cents would be equal to 155 cents.)

Then ask him to do the following calculations and give you the final total:

Multiply the number of cents by five
Add seven to the product
Multiply the total by four
Add nine to this product
Multiply by five and give you the answer

Once you receive the answer, you can immediately tell him how much money he has in cents. All you need to do is to cross out the two right hand numbers and subtract one from what you have left.

Let's look at an example. Suppose your friend has a penny, a dime and two nickels. This is equal to 21 cents.

$$21 \times 5 = 105$$
$$105 + 7 = 112$$
$$112 \times 4 = 448$$
$$448 + 9 = 457$$
$$457 \times 5 = 2285$$

Once you know the total, 2285, cross out the 8 and the 5 and subtract 1 from the remaining 22 to arrive at 21, the correct amount of change your friend has. This will always work, even if your friend has no (zero) money, or if he has $1,236,985.32 (which would be 123,698,532 cents, or 123 million, 698 thousand, 532 cents).

Why does it work? You will find the solution is easy if you have an interest in mathematics, but a few clues might aid you. Ignore the two steps of addition for a moment, and think about the rest of the procedure. You asked your friend to multiply by five, then by four, and then by five again. If you multiply four by five, and the product of this by five, you will get 100. In effect, you are having your friend multiply the "secret" number by 100. You have him do the multiplication in steps just to disguise this fact.

The numbers you have him add result only in increasing the total by a number that is more than 100, but less then 200. To solve the problem, then, you subtract 100 plus the number made by the last two digits of the final total. When you crossed those two digits out, you were really subtracting. If you will try doing this problem, using a variety of numbers to represent your friend's change, you can easily see how it works. Mathematical problems are usually more easily understood when you look at the numbers rather than read an explanation of them as words in a book.

Another, although not at all baffling, method would be to ask your friend to multiply his "cents" by 5, the product by 4, and the product of this by 5 again. To this total he should add 150 (a number between 100 and 200). You would be able to determine his change using the same method as above. If you look at the numbers, however, you will readily understand why your friend will probably not be fooled this time.

$$21 \times 5 \quad = \quad 105$$
$$105 \times 4 \quad = \quad 420$$
$$420 \times 5 \quad = 2100$$
$$2100 + 150 = 2250$$

Crossing out the right two figures from 2250, and subtracting 1 from remainder, leaves 21. You could also save your friend a good deal of arithmetic by simply asking him to multiply his figure by 100, and crossing out the two figures to the right to indicate his number.

To fool your friend, it must be difficult for him to guess how you knew his number just by knowing the total. The addition steps in the original experiment produced a total that did not show his actual number. Can you explain how including a 7 and a 9 as addition steps resulted in increasing the final figure by a number between one and two hundred? If the multiplication steps were 5, 4 and 10, (which would be equal to multiplying by 200 rather than 100) could you determine a method of telling how much change your friend had?

ODD AND EVEN

You can easily fool a friend who is good at mathematics several times with this simple trick. To solve it, he will have to think, both about arithmetic and about what you are saying.

Put a number of pennies in a dish. Now ask your friend to remove a few while your back is turned. When he has done this, you then reach into the dish and remove a few more. Then you tell him—"I will add my coins to yours. If the number you have taken is odd, mine will make an even total, and, if the number you have taken is even, mine will make it odd."

A Proper Match

Things Needed:
A dish
Some pennies

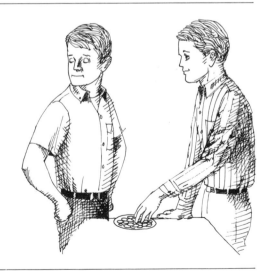

Have him count his coins. Continue the count with your coins. Sure enough, if he finishes counting his coins with an even total, you finish with an odd one! If he finishes with an odd total, you finish with an even one. You may repeat this many times, each time taking a different number of coins, and you always succeed. How many times must you do it before your friend guesses how it works?

Actually, even a good mathematician would probably have trouble at first. The answer is almost too simple. You can take any number of coins you wish each time, **as long as you take an odd number.**

Your odd number, added to your friend's even number, will make an odd total. Added to an odd number, the total will always be even, right?

TELEPHONE TRICKERY

Do you always think about what you are doing? When you are solving a math problem, do you use your brain to wonder why things are so, or simply as a calculating machine filled with numbers?

A scientist is sometimes referred to as a man who can "ask good questions." A question is asked when we do not understand what we are thinking about. For instance when you are solving a math problem, your brain often may be too busy arriving at a solution to have time to ask questions.

Do not be confused by this. It simply means that when you are solving one problem, you may be too busy to solve another at the same time. You can use your friend's mind to prove that this can happen.

By the Telephone

Things Needed:
A penny
A quarter

Tell your friend that you will call him on the telephone when he gets home. To prepare for your call, he should place a quarter and a penny on a table next to his telephone.

Later, when you call, you explain that you would like to do a magic trick for him. Tell him to place either the quarter or the penny in his pocket and leave the other one by the phone. Then say that you would like him to do a bit of arithmetic for you, but, from now on, he should say only the words "yes" or "okay" after he has finished each problem.

You then ask him to do the following things:

Look at the coin that is on the table.
Multiply the coin by 13.
Add 5 to this product.
Divide the total by 2, and remember the figure.
Multiply the coin in his pocket by 13.
Add 5 to this product.
Divide this total by 2, and remember the figure.

When he has finished the last step, you then tell him which coin he has in his pocket, and which is still on the table! This is sure to surprise him, because you haven't even asked him for an answer to your arithmetic problems. He may think it was a lucky guess; if so, ask him to put the coins back on the table, and do it again.

Before reading the explanation of this trick, perhaps you can solve it for yourself. Remember that his brain became too involved solving one puzzle to think about another one.

You give your friend a series of problems to solve. Each time you wait until your friend indicates, with "yes," that he has completed that step before you proceed to the next. He becomes very busy solving your problems, wondering what the next one will be, and trying to guess what the trick is. He's too busy to really question what he is doing.

You do not have his problems. You already know what is coming next and you do not have to do any mathematics. In fact, the answers to your math questions are not important! What is important? The way his brain solves the math problems.

Still confused? The only important problem you give him is to multiply the coin by 13. Think about this a moment before reading on. Can you see how this one question can let you decide which coin was where?

Naturally, when your friend finishes solving one of your questions, he will indicate with a "yes" that he is ready for the next. And it will take him longer to multiply a quarter by 13 than a penny!

All you have to do is listen closely after asking him to multiply each coin by 13. You will notice that in one case you receive a "yes" immediately and, in the other case, after a long pause. This will tell you which coin is the penny and which is the quarter.

Your friend will not be aware of this pause. He will be too busy solving the problem to think about how long it takes. You are free to notice just that, and take advantage of it.

Even after doing the experiment two times, your friend will probably still be bewildered by your ability. He will start to ask questions. However, now it is too late. Because his mind has been so involved with mathematics, he will be sure that the solution must lie in the arithmetic. This will confuse him still further because you never asked for an answer to any of the problems.

You probably won't be able to do the trick more than twice. On the third try your friend will remember how much 25×13 is, and will not pause. Two tries will work; even on the second try he will pause to remember the answer. You might try changing to another number (17, for instance), but this will probably give him the clue that the numbers themselves aren't important.

Your brain is a complex tool. It works for you in many different ways. It recalls facts, solves problems, makes comparisons, relates ideas, and does all the other things we call thinking. It also has the ability to concentrate completely on what it is doing. This lets us get things done by screening out distractions, but it is also the way magicians commonly fool us, causing us to concentrate on one thing while they are doing something quite different.

RIGHT OR LEFT

If your friend guesses the solution to your telephone trick, try this one on him the next time. Instead of pauses, it depends on straight arithmetic. It works because most people look for a trick rather than bothering to think about the experiment. Like the last, this trick can be done over the telephone.

A Coin in the Hand

Things Needed:
A penny
A dime

Give your friend a penny and a dime. Ask him to hold the penny in one hand and the dime in the other, without letting you know which is which. Then have him do a little simple arithmetic for you. Have him multiply the value of the coin in his right hand by 2, 4, or 6, and remember the answer. Then have him multiply the value of the coin in his left hand by 1, 3, or 5. (In both cases he has a free choice of which number to use as the multiplier.) Then ask him to add the two answers together and give you the total. You can then tell him which hand each of the coins is in.

We generally think about pennies and dimes as coins, and not as numbers. Actually, a dime is the even number 10, while the penny is the odd number 1. It is because one value is even, while the other is odd, that this trick works.

You will notice that you first ask that the coin in the right hand be multiplied by an even number. If the coin is even (the dime), the product will be even. If it is the odd coin (the penny), the product will also be even.

But you multiply by an odd number on the left hand. Therefore, if that hand has the dime, the product will be even, but if it has the penny, the product will be odd. It is the product of the left hand that gives you your clue. When the products are added together, the total will be odd only if the left-hand product is odd; and that will happen only if the left hand holds the penny!

Because of this difference, all you have to know is whether the answer your friend gives you is even or odd. If odd, the penny is in the left hand; if even, the dime is in the left hand.

PLAYING WITH PROBABILITY

There are about 200 million people in this country. About 200 of them will be struck by lightning during the coming year. What are your chances of being hit by lightning this year? By dividing the number of people in the country by the number hit, we can say that the odds are about one million to one against your being hit. That is, one person out of a million will be struck by lightning this year. These are very good odds.

If you flip a coin with a friend, what are your odds if you choose heads? There are two sides to a coin. You have chosen one side, so your odds are one in two, or fifty-fifty.

Whenever we ask questions like these two, we are involved in the study of probability. It is one of the most fascinating fields of mathematics.

All of the things that we call luck, or chance, can be numerically calculated in terms of probability. Will you get a new bike for your birthday? Will your baseball team win its next game? What are the chances that your school will burn down? Will your sister be nice to you throughout the day? If you had enough information, you could calculate the chances of all these things. But, unfortunately, the information you would require is probably unavailable.

A PROBABILITY PROBLEM

Suppose that you and two friends are trying to choose who will be the next captain of your baseball team. Someone suggests that you toss two coins for it. One of you will choose two heads, one will choose two tails, and one will choose a head and a tail. Whichever combination comes up when the coins are tossed will determine the next captain. Which combination will you choose?

A knowledge of probability will give you an advantage over your friends. You may be surprised to learn that one of these combinations is twice as good as either of the other two.

You can decide which is the best choice with a simple experiment. Divide a piece of paper into three columns. Label them "two heads", "two tails" and "head/tail". Now flip two pennies one hundred times. Record which combination comes up each time by making a mark in the appropriate column. When you have completed one hundred tosses, which column has more marks?

A less time-consuming method of deciding which combination is the wisest choice is to consider the mathematics of the experiment. First, notice that you can only get the head combination in one way, head/head. Both coins must come up showing a head. The tail combination, also, must be tail/tail. However, the last combination may be a head/tail or a tail/head. Hence, there is only one way to get head/head, or tail/tail, but there are two different ways to get a head and a tail. Therefore if you choose the head/tail combination, you will have a fifty-fifty chance while your friends will share a fifty-fifty chance between them, thus giving them each a quarter of a chance. In other words, half the time the coins will come up either two heads and two tails, and the rest of the time either head/tail or tail/head. This gives you twice as good a chance as either of your friends.

You cannot count on this method to guarantee that you will be the next captain of your baseball team, however, for two reasons. The first is that the odds will work out perfectly only over a great many throws. If you flip two coins one hundred times, the head/tail combination should come up exactly fifty times, while the two heads and the two tails should come up exactly twenty-five times each . . . but this is extremely unlikely with such a limited number of trials. To have the odds show up perfectly you would have to flip the coins many thousands of times. When you are flipping one coin, the head side might come up three times in a row; only after a great number of throws would it be obvious that your odds are truly fifty-fifty. In any one throw, it's all up to chance, and mathematics can only tell you when the odds are in, or out of, your favor.

Secondly, in deciding the captaincy, remember that your odds are two to one in favor of beating each of your partners, because each of the others has one-fourth of the odds. But your two partners together have half the odds—which means that your odds of winning over both of them will be fifty-fifty, exactly the same as if you flipped a single coin with one friend. Your two partners are at a greater disadvantage. Each of them will have one chance in four to become team captain, while your chances will be one in two.

Even if you lose, you may find comfort in the fact that mathematics is on your side. If you continued to flip in this way, over many years, you would spend one-half the time as captain of the team, while your friends would share the other half, each serving one-quarter of the time.

SPELLING COINS

Do you know that each coin can spell its own name?

Educated Coins

Things Needed:
A penny
A nickel
A quarter
A dime

Arrange the coins in a line on the table in this order: penny, nickel, quarter and dime. Be sure that they are in just this order.

Ask a friend to spell any one of the coin's names. He should start at the left, tapping the penny for the first letter, the nickel for the second, and so forth. If he reaches the end of the line and has not finished spelling, he should make his next tap on the penny at the start of the row.

When he finishes the last letter, his finger will be resting on the coin he has been spelling! Let him try it again, using another coin. He will find that every one of the coins "knows its name."

If you play with coins long enough, you will begin to feel that they are old friends, and that each one has its own personality. Despite this feeling, however, coins do not actually have any intelligence. The intelligence in this trick must be supplied by you.

The mathematics is very simple. If you write down the names of the four coins, you will discover an interesting fact. "Dime" contains four letters, "penny" five, "nickel" six, and "quarter" seven. Each name has just one more letter than the one before it.

If we arrange the line so that the dime falls in fourth place, it is very easy to then place the penny in fifth, the nickel in sixth and the quarter in seventh.

Once you know the simple formula it is possible to arrange the coins in slightly different ways and still get the right answers. Adding more coins can make the arrangement look less deliberate.

Will this work?

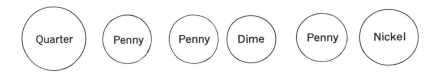

Now try arranging the coins in other ways.

IT'S A DATE

Before reading the solution, can you figure out how this math-magic trick could be done?

I give you six pennies, each with a different date. I ask you to remember any one of the dates you like, and return the pennies to me. I lay three pennies on the table and ask if you see your date among them. You answer "yes". I lay three others down and again you see your date. Now I can tell you the date you are thinking of.

We try it again. This time you do not see your penny the second time but, again, I can tell you the date on the coin in your mind.

How can I "read your mind" every time we conduct this problem? I do it by using *cross reference*, a method that is used to determine an unknown object by simply eliminating all other objects.

If a scientist has an unknown powdery green chemical, with certain characteristics, he will probably use cross-reference to identify it. He knows that it is a powder, so he eliminates all gases and liquids. He also eliminates all chemicals which are not green. By further comparisons he will be left with only one chemical which is just like his. Now he knows his chemical's name.

So, by using cross-reference, you can identify an unknown date on a coin and appear to read your friend's mind.

Pick a Date

Things Needed:
Six pennies, each with a different date

Arrange the pennies by their dates so that the oldest is first and the newest last. This will make it easier to remember which number each date represents. First, you will have to give each date a number, and take the time to remember them.

For example:

1940—#1	1956—#3	1960—#5
1952—#2	1958—#4	1968—#6

Now hand the pennies to your friend. After he has chosen one date to remember, he returns them to you. You separate them into groups of three each. In

Group I put pennies 1, 2, and 3. Put 4, 5, and 6 in Group II.

Place Group I on the table. Ask if his date is among them. His answer will eliminate one of the Groups. If he sees his penny you know it is not one of Group II and you can concentrate on Group I.

Now, you could put two of the Group I pennies down and ask him if his date is among them. If he answered "yes" you would then remove one of them and ask again. But this method would be far too obvious. However, if you understand this process of elimination you can easily make it a bit more complicated and confuse your friend.

Suppose he answers "yes" when you first put down Group I. You now know that it is either penny number 1, 2, or 3. The next three you put down should contain any two of these plus one penny from Group II. (You know the Group II penny is not his). If he does not see his penny this time you know that his penny is the one from Group I which you did **not** put on the table. This is where your memorizing comes in.

If he does see it, you know that it is one of the two Group I pennies on the table. The next three you put down should contain either one of these Group I pennies, plus two from Group II.

If he does not see his penny this time it must have been the Group I penny you eliminated. If he does see it, it must be the only penny from Group I remaining on the table.

If words confuse you, let's see how it appears in numbers. Let's assume that your friend has selected penny number 2.

First you put down Group I:

(He sees his penny, number 2.)

Next you eliminate a penny from Group I and substitute any penny from Group II. Let's use number 6.

(He still sees his penny, number 2.)

On your third try you eliminate penny number 2, and substitute another from Group II. We'll use number 5.

(This time he does not see his penny, number 2.)

You now know that it must have been the last one you eliminated from Group I. This was number 2!

Another way of understanding how cross-reference and elimination solve this trick is to study a *key*. This is a process which does the work for you. It is often used by scientists to identify unknown plants or animals. A "key" to the penny puzzle would read like this:

A) Lay down pennies 1, 2, and 3 (Group I)
    If he does not see his penny do step (B).
    If he does see his penny . . .
        Lay down any penny from Group II, plus numbers 2 and 3.
        If he does not see his penny, **it is number 1.**
        If he does see his penny . . .
            Lay down any 2 pennies from Group II, plus penny number 3.
            If he sees his penny, **it is number 3.**
            If not, **it is number 2.**

B) Lay down any penny from Group I, plus numbers 5 and 6.
    If he does not see his penny, **it is number 4.**
    If he does see his penny . . .
        Lay down any two pennies from Group I, plus number 6.
        If he does see his penny, **it is number 6.**
        If he does not see it, **it is number 5.**

Using this key, you will never have to lay pennies more than three times, often fewer times.

It will take you a bit of time to memorize which dates are represented by numbers 1 through 6; however, once you have done this you will find that you can do the trick quickly. The faster you lay down coins, seemingly at random, the more puzzled your friend will be.

Be sure to put the coins down in a different order each time so that your friend will not see any pattern to them.

Now, try working out a method for giving your friend a choice from a group of nine pennies, or more.

6

Final Fun-damentals

Let's finish up with a variety of investigations. Some will be seemingly impossible stunts, some will fool your friends, and one or two may even surprise you. Some you can do right away and others will require you to do a bit of investigating and deep thinking on your own.

To start your brain working, here are a few coin-quickies for you to solve:

- If you look carefully through your change, you might find one coin with a date that reads the same upside down and right side up. Can you find it? (Perhaps you can think of it without looking.)

- Suppose you place two pennies on the table so that the heads of Abraham Lincoln are touching each other. You then roll one penny around the other. How many times will Abraham Lincoln turn upside down as he rolls once around the other penny? Even if you try this, be careful before you answer!

• Can you place four pennies on the table in such a way as to make every one of the pennies touch every other one? It's not as easy as it sounds: try it!

• Before you try this next one, guess at the answer. How many pennies will fit around the outside of a single penny so that each one touches the central one? How many nickels will fit around a central nickel? Quarters? Try them all and you'll be surprised.

SEEING THE SUN WHEN THE SUN CAN'T BE SEEN

This tongue twisting title is actually an introduction to a fact that you have probably observed already, though you may never have realized it.

As the day draws to a close, the sun sinks slowly in the west until it is completely hidden by the horizon. If you look westward, just before it drops out of sight, you may be surprised to know that the sun is not where it appears to be. It may be completely hidden by the horizon for several minutes in spite of the fact that you can still see it.

Do not be confused. Remember, you do not actually see the sun at any time. What you do see is the light that is coming from it.

When the sun drops below the horizon it is completely out of your sight. However, the rays of light from it are streaming through the air overhead. These rays have traveled through about 93 million miles of space in a straight line from the sun to the earth. When the rays strike the heavy atmosphere of the earth, they are suddenly bent downward. Imagine a bullet fired from a gun into a pond. The bullet travels straight through the air to the water, but bends downward once it strikes the denser water.

Because the light rays bend downward, your eyes, seeing them as an image of the sun, will observe the sun to be higher in the sky than it actually is.

Here is an experiment you might perform to prove that light rays are easily bent, and can cause something to appear where it isn't.

A Coin You Can't See

Things Needed:
A coin
A soup bowl
A pitcher of water

Place the coin in the center of the soup bowl. You can see the coin because the light, reflecting from it, is entering your eye.

Bend down until the coin is just hidden from your view by the edge of the bowl. The rim prevents light from the coin from entering your eye.

While you hold your head still in this position, have a friend fill the bowl with water. The coin will mysteriously reappear and you will be able to see it plainly.

The coin is really still hidden by the edge of the bowl, but the denser water bends the light rays reflecting from the coin. The bent rays now enter your eye and you see an image of the coin in a different place than it actually is. Now mentally substitute the sun for the coin, the horizon for the edge of the soup bowl, and the atmosphere for the water, and you can readily understand how it is possible to see the sun when the sun can't be seen.

MAKING NOTHING OUT OF SOMETHING

If light did not reflect off your body, what would you look like? A friend would see only a black, shadowlike "hole" in the shape of a person! The only way we see anything is to have light enter our eyes. Without light we would be blind, and an object that did not reflect light into our eyes would be impossible to see as anything but black. Fortunately, everything seems to reflect some light, and it is highly doubtful that anyone will ever appear in this way. But you can make a coin impossible to see, by causing its reflected light to bend away from your eyes.

An Invisible Coin

Things Needed:
A coin
A *straight-sided* glass filled with water
A saucer

Place the coin on the table. Fill the glass to the top with water and rest it on the coin. Place the saucer on top of the glass. Can you see the coin? Now lift off the saucer and look. When you remove the saucer you will be able to see the coin only by looking down from the top. If you remove the water, you will be able to see it through the sides of the glass, too. Obviously the water is the "magic" in this investigation.

Without the water, light from the coin comes through the sides of the glass; but when the water is added, the light rays are bent upward. None of the coin's reflected light comes out the sides, so the coin is invisible when you look through the sides.

Naturally, light is still reflecting off the coin. To prevent this light from reaching your eyes, you place a saucer on top of the glass. The light rays strike the bottom of the saucer and cannot reach your eye. The coin is as hidden from view as if you had placed a saucer directly on top of it.

Because it is impossible to see any of the coin's reflected light, you cannot see it ... no matter how hard you look, or how well you know it is still there. It is invisible!

HOW TO BE GENEROUS WITHOUT LOSING A CENT

"You can't have your cake and eat it too" is a very old saying. Here is an investigation that lets you appear to do just that. You can offer your friend some money, and still keep it for yourself . . . although he is perfectly free to take it if he can.

Place a penny and a dime on a table. Tell your friend that you will give him one . . . but he must decide which one he will take. You will make just one condition which he must agree to:

. . . that if what you are about to say is true, he can take the dime

. . . and that if it is false, he can take the penny.

Can you think of something to say that will make it impossible for him to take either coin? As you think about this puzzle you are becoming involved in the use of logic. Logic is an important tool for a scientist.

An Impossible Offer

Things Needed:
A penny
A dime

If certain things are true and you decide, because of these things, that something else will have to occur, your decision is "logical." For example, if you notice that children grow into adults, you should know, by logic, that you will be an adult one day also. Or, if a scientist notices that when two chemicals are mixed together a gas is produced, he might decide, logically, that the chemicals contain all the right ingredients to make that particular gas.

What you should say to your friend must be logical, too. You can decide what to say by carefully studying the problem and the rules. Remember, he can take the dime if what you say is true. If you say, "You can take the dime," he will! These two statements fit perfectly together, and it is logical for him to take the dime.

Also, you cannot say, "You must not take the penny." In this case he can abide by your statements and take either the dime or the penny. Do you see why?

If you understand this reasoning, you are solving the problem by logic. You can see how two statements may agree, or disagree, with one another. Recognizing this is the first step to logical thinking. As you grow older, you will often find it necessary to make decisions. You will use your past experience to decide what should be done in the future. Naturally, what you do in the future must agree and work well with what has been done in the past. To be successful, your final decision must be based on logic.

To solve the penny and dime puzzle you must find a statement that will not agree with either your true or your false one.

"You must take the penny."

If that is true, he can take the dime . . . but if he does take it your statement will become false.   If the statement is false, he can take the penny . . . but if he does that, your statement would turn out to be true (which means he must take the dime).   What can he do? Absolutely nothing!   There is no way that your final statement can be made to agree with your true and false ones.

You could also say, "You must not take the dime." Can you see why?

A Final Problem in Logic.   Suppose your friend has two coins in his pocket.   Added together, these two coins make fifteen cents.   One is not a dime. Can you tell what the two coins are?

TUMBLING DIMES AND STICKY PENNIES

Place a dime, with the head side up, flat on a table.   Ask a friend to hold his hands behind his back and, while doing this, turn the dime over so that the tail side shows.

Make a Dime Flip Its Head

Things Needed:
A dime

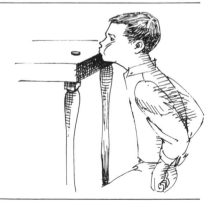

He obviously can't use his hands, and he must not touch the dime in any way.

At first he may feel that it is impossible. Eventually, he will probably suggest that the only way to meet your challenge is by blowing the dime over. You tell him that's exactly what you had in mind all along. He has solved the problem . . . but now let's see him do it! He will do quite a bit of blowing, all to no avail, and will finally challenge you to show him how.

Place the dime, head side up, flat on a table and about six inches from the edge. Bend down so your head is even with the tabletop and blow hard across the table **over** the dime. It will do a somersault and land tail side up!

As hard as your friend tries, he will be unable to make the coin move if he blows down on it. Blowing downward only presses the dime harder against the table. Why does it work easily when you blow sidewise at it?

Naturally this is an investigation of air, but, more specifically, it is an investigation of air *pressure.*

Although air is invisible, there is an awful lot of it around. We live at the bottom of a great ocean of air. Air is pressing down with nearly 15 pounds of pressure on every square inch of surface. A dime has nearly eight pounds of air on top of it! When you blow down on it, you are increasing this pressure even more.

But let's look inside that moving stream of air. There is a simple rule of science which states that moving air will exert less pressure than non-moving air. Every moving stream of air can therefore be considered a low-pressure area, where the pressure is less than 15 pounds per square inch.

When you blow over the dime, you produce a low-pressure area just above the coin. The heavier, non-moving air under the dime pushes the coin upward into this low-pressure stream. As it moves upward, the moving air gives it a slight spin which causes it to flip. If you could continue blowing, the dime would remain "floating" above the tabletop. Magicians frequently cause things to appear to "float in the air." For a brief moment you have done the same . . . except that you used the air, and a bit of science, rather than magic to aid you.

Because the air is heavy, and exerts pressure on everything on earth, you can use the air to stick a penny on your forehead.

Touch a finger to your tongue and rub a bit of the saliva on a penny. Press the moistened side of the coin hard against your forehead. Remove your finger, and the coin will cling to your head.

Tip your head forward. Does the coin fall off? Shake your head; wrinkle your brow. How hard is it to make the penny fall off?

A Sticky Trick

Things Needed:
A penny

Can you guess why the penny clings so tightly? You might suspect it is because the saliva is sticky. Try the investigation again, using a dry penny. It will also stick, but probably not so tightly.

Again, air pressure is the "magic" to this trick. When you hold a penny the pressure is pushing down from the top, but it is also pushing up from the bottom and at the sides. With pressure all around, we are not aware of the weight of the air. When you press the coin to your head, you squeeze the air out from underneath. With less air underneath to press out, the air on the outside presses harder against the coin. The coin is held on your head by the weight of the air; the saliva only helps to make a better air seal.

This investigation is quite a bit like the one of the flipping dime. The dime was pushed from an area of high pressure to an area of low pressure. The sticky penny is pushed in the same way, but your head gets in the way so the penny is pushed tightly against your skin.

DO YOU LOOK WITHOUT SEEING?

An observer notices the small things, the beautiful things, and the special things about whatever he looks at. He sees things quite differently from a person who is not an observer. Now what about you? Do you just look at things, or are you an observer?

You can find out quickly by trying to answer the questions below. If you get most of the answers right you are probably a careful observer. If you cannot answer many, perhaps you are not looking carefully enough, and you will have to do just that to find out.

1. The most common penny has a picture of Abraham Lincoln on it. Is he facing right or left?
2. Is he wearing any kind of necktie?
3. Does the penny say "one cent" or "1¢" on it?
4. Which United States coins have milled (rough) edges?
5. Is the back of a coin right side up or upside down in relation to the front side?
6. There are three phrases, and a single word, that appear on all United States coins being made today. Can you remember what they are?
7. Which coin is thicker, a nickel or a quarter?
8. Old nickels had a picture of a buffalo on the back. Can you name an animal that appears on a present-day coin?
9. You can find pictures of some of the presidents on coins. Pennies show Abraham Lincoln, dimes show Franklin Roosevelt, quarters show George Washington, and half dollars show John F. Kennedy. Whose face can you find on a nickel?
10. Two of these presidents are wearing wigs tied with a ribbon. Who are they?

NOW IT'S UP TO YOU

There are still many things to do with coins. It is surprising how many things coins can be used for besides spending. Their size, shape, color, and material often make them just the right objects with which to do an investigation. Now it is up to you to invent some coin investigations of your own. Here are some ideas to start you thinking:

- If a penny and a dime were left for an hour in the hot sun, which one would feel warmer?

- If a penny were left overnight in a refrigerator freezer, then dropped on a table, would it make the same sound or a different sound than a dropped penny that had been sitting in the sun?

- Nickel is a harder metal than either copper or silver. Can you prove it by using coins, without damaging them? What would be your proof?

- If a polished penny were set aside, how long would it take before it turned dark again? Would it happen faster if it were left inside or outside? (Use copper cleaner to shine the penny.)

- If you had a stack of pennies, could you find out how thick *one* penny is, without using a ruler? Hint: one penny is $\frac{3}{4}$ of an inch *wide*.

Does it surprise you that a whole book of science investigations in which coins are used could be written? To many people, science is just a lot of complicated machines, investigations, and experiments they feel they could never understand. But science is not "made" in laboratories. It is a constant part of our everyday life. We can't get away from it; in fact, we all use and depend on it every single day. This book was written to remind you of just this, and hopefully you will remember it every time you take out a coin to spend.

Index

Acetic acid, 37
Air pressure, 87–90
Alloys, 30–35, 38, 41–42
Ammonia, 37–38

Bending light rays, 81–84
Blind spot, 20–23
Brass, 32, 34–35

Camera, eye compared to, 8
Carbon, 32
Chemical compounds, 35
Chemical energy, 43–45
Chemical reactions:
    cleaning copper, 38
    corrosion of copper, 36–38
    corrosion of iron, 35–36
    in eye cells, 19, 23
    silver sulphide (tarnish), 39–40
Chemical tests for silver, 39–40
Chlorine, 37
Clad coins, 42
Coins, history of, 29
Compounds, chemical, 35

Copper, 31–32, 34–38, 41–42
    corrosion of, 36–38
Copper chloride, 37–38
Copper hydroxide, 38
Copper sulphate, 37–38
Corrosion, 35–38
Cross reference, 75

Depth, 18
Detergent soap, 7
Distance deception, 26–28
Double vision, 16–17

Eclipse, 27
Energy, 43–51, 53–56
    atomic, 43
    chemical, 43–45
    electrical, 43
    heat, 43–45, 49
    kinetic, 44
    light, 43
    mechanical, 43–45, 49
    potential, 44

sound, 43, 49
  transfer of, 45–50
Eye, 8–26
  functioning of, 15, 17, 22–26
  nerves in, 19–20
  structure of, 8, 13, 19–20, 22

Fovea, 13–16
Friction, 48–49, 52, 57

Galvanizing, 32–33
Gold, 29
Gravity, 58–59

Heat energy, 43–45, 49
History of metal money, 29
Hydrogen, 37–38

Image, size varies with distance,
  22, 26
Inertia, 50–56
Invisible coin, 84
Iron, 32–33, 35–36
Iron oxide, 36

Key, 78–79
Kinetic energy, 44

Laminating, 42
Laws of motion, 49–53, 58
Light, bending of rays, 81–84
  needed for seeing, 9
  reflection of, 83–84
Lightning, 70
Logic, 85–87
Lustre, 35, 42

Magnetic coin, 33–34
Manganese, 41
Mass, 54
Matches, 39

Mechanical energy, 43–45, 49
Metal money, history of, 29
Molecules, water, 6
Momentum, 53–57
Moon, size in relation to sun, 26
Motion, 23, 43
  laws of, 49–53, 58
  straight-line, 58–59
Mustard, 40

Nerves, in eye, 19–20
Newton, Sir Isaac, 49–50, 58

Observation, 90–91
Odd and even, 64–65
Optic nerve, 20
Optical illusions, 8–28, 81–84
Orbit, 58–59
Oxygen, 35, 37–38

Peanut butter quarter, 41–42
Pendulum, 48
Persistence of vision, 23–26
Potential energy, 44
Pressure, air, 87–90
Probability, 70–73

Reflection of light, 83–84
Retina, 8–9, 19
Rust, 35–38

Satellites, 58–59
Shell case coppers, 34
Silver (element), 39–41
  chemical tests for, 39–41
Silver nickel (coin), 41
Silver sulphide, 39–40
Size, recognition of, 10–13,
  26–28
Speed, 55

Stainless steel, 39
Steel, 32–34, 39
Straight-line motion, 58–59
Sulphur, 39–41
   in household substances,
      40–41
   in matches, 39
   in mustard, 40
Sun, light rays, 81–82
   size in relation to moon, 26
Surface tension, 6–7

Tarnish, 39–40
Telephone, 66, 69
Tension, surface, 6–7

Tests for silver, 39–41
Three-dimensional vision, 17–18
Tin, 31, 35
Transfer of energy, 45–50
Two eyes, significance of, 17–18

Velocity, 55
Vinegar, 36–38
Vision, persistence of, 23–26

Water level, 5–6
Water molecules, 6
Wetting agent, 7
Work, 43

Zinc, 32–33, 35

ABOUT THE AUTHOR

Laurence B. White, Jr., is a member in good standing of the Society of American Magicians, but the kind of "magic" he likes best is science. As Assistant Director of the Needham (Massachusetts) Elementary Science Center, former Supervisor of Programs and Courses at the Boston Museum of Science, and as a popular television teacher he has specialized in dramatic presentations of scientific ideas. He carries this (literally) into his private life as well, with a pocketful of Canadian nickels always handy for experiments with magnetism. A native of Massachusetts, he now lives in Stoughton with his wife and two sons.